About Skill Builders
Reading
Comprehension Grade 6

Welcome to Skill Builders *Reading Comprehension* for sixth grade. This book is designed to improve children's reading comprehension skills through focused practice. The book's eye-catching graphics and engaging topics entice even reluctant readers. Each full-color workbook contains grade-level-appropriate passages and exercises based on national standards to help ensure that children master basic skills before progressing.

More than 70 pages of activities cover essential comprehension strategies, such as inferring, sequencing, and finding the main idea and supporting details. The workbook also contains questions and activities to help children build their vocabularies.

The Skill Builders series offers workbooks that are perfect for keeping children current during the school year or preparing them for the next grade.

Credits:
Content Editor: Elizabeth Swenson
Copy Editor: Carrie D'Ascoli
Layout, Cover Design, and Inside Illustrations: Nick Greenwood

www.carsondellosa.com
Carson-Dellosa Publishing LLC
Greensboro, North Carolina

ISBN 978-1-936023-34-9
15-210191151

Table of Contents

Suggested Reading List

Aiken, Joan
The Wolves of Willoughby Chase

Armstrong, Jennifer
Shipwreck at the Bottom of the World: The Extraordinary True Story of Shackleton and the Endurance

Bloor, Edward
Tangerine

Byers, Betsy
The Pinballs

Clement-Davies, David
Fire Bringer

Craven, Margaret
I Heard the Owl Call My Name

Cushman, Karen
Catherine, Called Birdy

DiCamillo, Kate
The Tale of Despereaux

Durbin, William
The Broken Blade

Eckert, Allan W.
Incident at Hawk's Hill

Fast, Howard
April Morning

Fleischman, John
Phineas Gage: A Gruesome but True Story about Brain Science

Freedman, Russell
Out of Darkness: The Story of Louis Braille

Greene, Bette
Summer of My German Soldier

Gutman, Dan
Jackie & Me

Henkes, Kevin
Words of Stone

Hesse, Karen
Stowaway

Hiaasen, Carl
Flush; Hoot

Hinton, S. E.
The Outsiders

Korman, Gordon
I Want to Go Home!; The Twinkie Squad

Lindgren, Astrid
Pippi Longstocking

Lowry, Lois
Number the Stars; The Giver

McKinley, Robin
The Blue Sword

Montgomery, L. M.
Anne of Green Gables

Murphy, Glenn
Inventions

Myers, Walter Dean
The Outside Shot

O'Dell, Scott
The Black Pearl

Paterson, Katherine
Bridge to Terabithia

Paulsen, Gary
The Island; Hatchet

Pullman, Philip
The Golden Compass

Rawls, Wilson
Where the Red Fern Grows

Rubin, Robert Alden
Poetry Out Loud

Sleator, William
House of Stairs

Snyder, Zilpha Keatley
The Egypt Game; Velvet Room

Spinelli, Jerry
Maniac Magee; Wringer

Stewart, Trenton Lee
The Mysterious Benedict Society

Taylor, Mildred D.
Roll of Thunder, Hear My Cry

Walker, Niki
Generating Wind Power

Walsh, Jill Paton
The Green Book

White, Ruth
Belle Prater's Boy

The First Ice-Cream Cone

Read the passage. Then, answer the questions.

Americans have been enjoying ice-cream cones for more than 100 years. The invention of the ice-cream cone is credited to Italo Marchiony, an Italian immigrant in New York City. Marchiony owned a pushcart, which he used to sell lemon ice on the sidewalks of New York. His first cone was made of paper. He then created a cone made from pastry that could be eaten. It became so popular that he applied for a **patent** on his edible cone. The patent made it illegal for anyone else to make an edible cone exactly like the one he designed.

Although Marchiony is credited with the invention of the ice-cream cone, a similar creation was developed independently in 1904 at the St. Louis World's Fair. People came to the fair from all over the world. A man named Charles Menches had a stand where he sold ice cream in dishes.

According to a version of the story, one day at the fair, Menches ran out of dishes. It was very warm, and he still had several hours of business ahead of him. A nearby vendor, Ernest Hamwi, was selling a fritter-like treat called *zalabia*. Zalabia is a crisp pastry sold with syrup. Menches asked if he could borrow some of the zalabia. He rolled one and scooped ice cream on top. Menches's cone with ice cream became an instant hit, and the ice-cream cone was born a second time.

1. Which of the following best defines the word **patent**?

  A. a committee that rates the usefulness of new products

  B. a loan used to start a business

  C. a notebook used to record ideas

  D. an exclusive right or license to make and sell a product

2. Write *T* if the statement is true. Write *F* if the statement is false.

  _____ Marchiony sold ice cream in St. Louis.

  _____ Hamwi sold ice cream in New York City.

  _____ Menches sold lemon ice in New York City.

  _____ Menches began using zalabia as a dish for ice cream.

3. Which best identifies the time setting of the passage?

  A. early 1800s

  B. late 1800s

  C. early twentieth century

  D. late twentieth century

4. Explain the main idea of this passage.

  _____

  _____

  _____

  _____

  _____

Queen Lili'uokalani

Read the passage. Then, answer the questions.

Lili'uokalani (li-lē-e-wō-ka-lä-nē) was not born a queen. She was born Lydia Kamaka'eha. When her brother was crowned the king of Hawaii in 1874, she was a princess. In 1881, the king left on a long trip and put Lili'uokalani in charge of Hawaii while he was gone. Then, disaster struck in Hawaii. A terrible disease, smallpox, arrived.

Lili'uokalani acted quickly. She discovered that some workers from China had brought the sickness to Hawaii, so she closed the ports. This made Americans who shipped sugar from the Hawaiian islands very angry. But, Lili'uokalani cared only about her people and their ability to get well.

The king died in 1891, and Lili'uokalani became queen. Queen Lili'uokalani wanted to change American laws that took away her power as queen. She wanted to use that power to take care of her people and give them more rights. The Americans remembered when Lili'uokalani closed the ports and feared she might do that again. So, in 1893, the Americans took over. President Grover Cleveland tried to stop them, but he learned that Queen Lili'uokalani planned to punish the Americans. So instead, Hawaii became a **republic** of the United States. In 1895, Queen Lili'uokalani was arrested and imprisoned in her palace.

Queen Lili'uokalani was freed in 1896 and lived the rest of her life in Hawaii. Hawaii was annexed, or added, to the United States in 1898. In 1959, Hawaii achieved statehood. Today, Hawaiians remember Queen Lili'uokalani for her strong leadership.

1. Which of the following is another good title for the passage?

   A. A Queen in Prison
   B. Hawaii
   C. The Last Queen of Hawaii
   D. A New State

2. Which of the following best defines the word **republic**?

   A. something that belongs to the public
   B. a type of ruler
   C. a territory ruled by another country
   D. a kind of crime

3. Number the following events in the order in which they happened.

   _____ Hawaiians remember Queen Lili'uokalani for her strong leadership.

   _____ Lili'uokalani became queen.

   _____ Hawaii became a republic.

   _____ Lili'uokalani closed Hawaii's ports to protect the people from smallpox.

   _____ Lili'uokalani's brother left her in charge of Hawaii while he was traveling.

4. Who ruled Hawaii before Lili'uokalani?

   _____

5. Where was Lili'uokalani held prisoner?

   _____

Types of Government

Read the passage. Then, use words from the passage to complete the sentences.

Many models of government exist in the world. Governments are classified based on who has power and how limited the power is. Two types of government are totalitarian and democratic.

In a totalitarian government, a country's leaders have unlimited power. Totalitarian leaders often take their power by force. They keep tight control over their countries and people. Types of totalitarian governments include monarchy (rule by one person of royalty), oligarchy (rule by a small, select group of people), and dictatorship (rule by one person or political party).

Democratic governments give decision-making power to the people. The two types of democracies are direct and indirect (or representative). In a direct democracy, the people vote on and make laws. In an indirect democracy, the people elect representatives to make laws for them. Indirect democracies can be presidential or parliamentary. In a presidential system, like in the United States, the people elect a president. The president leads the executive branch of government. Members of a separate branch of government make the laws. This is the legislative branch.

In a parliamentary system, like in Great Britain, a political party leads the government. The head of that party becomes the prime minister. The prime minister is similar to a president. They both lead the executive branch. However, the prime minister is also part of the legislative branch.

1. The leaders of a _____ government have unlimited power.

2. _____ governments give the power to the people.

3. Great Britain has a _____ system of indirect democracy.

4. A monarchy is ruled by one person of _____.

5. Two types of democracies are _____ and _____.

6. A government ruled by a small, select group of people is called an _____.

7. One person or political party rules a _____.

8. The leader of a parliamentary democracy is called the _____.

9. In a _____ democracy, the people make the laws themselves.

10. Members of the _____ branch make the laws in a presidential system.

Grantland Rice—Beloved Sportswriter

Read the passage. Then, answer the questions.

Grantland Rice was one of America's best-loved sportswriters. He had a vast knowledge of many sports, and he wrote **eloquently** about them. But, what distinguished Rice from other sportswriters was the way he reported sports. He believed that good sportsmanship could lift people to morally greater heights. His philosophy of life became evident in his writing.

Rice was a columnist, a poet, and an author. He was also a film producer, a family man, a war veteran, and a skillful golfer. His personal accomplishments as a sportswriter spanned 50 years. Through Grantland Rice's words, good athletes became heroes. He made household names of athletes such as Ty Cobb, Jim Thorpe, and Red Grange. He wrote about Babe Didrikson Zaharias, Babe Ruth, and the "Four Horsemen" of Notre Dame. Grantland Rice honed the craft of sportswriting.

Rice often used poetry in his columns. Rice's most famous quotation came from the last two lines of his poem "Alumnus Football": "For when the One Great Scorer comes to mark against your name, He writes—not that you won or lost—but how you played the Game."

His death in 1954 was mourned across the United States, but Grantland Rice has not been forgotten. Since 1954, each year the national champions in college football are awarded the Grantland Rice Trophy.

1. What made Grantland Rice one of America's favorite sportswriters?
    A. He had a vast knowledge of many sports.
    B. He reported sports with a focus on good sportsmanship.
    C. Through his writing, he made American heroes out of good athletes.
    D. all of the above

2. Which of the following do you think would have been most important to Grantland Rice on the field of play?
    A. the final score
    B. good sportsmanship
    C. evenly matched teams
    D. a close game

3. Which of the following best defines the word **eloquently**?
    A. unfavorably
    B. expressively
    C. recognizably
    D. not very cleverly

4. Which best characterizes the time setting for the sportswriting career of Grantland Rice?
    A. early 1800s
    B. late 1800s
    C. early twentieth century
    D. late twentieth century

5. How do you think the final two lines of Rice's poem "Alumnus Football" reflect the way Rice felt about competitive sports?

_____

_____

_____

Mason and Dixon

Read the passage. Then, answer the questions.

Many people today associate the Mason-Dixon Line with the American Civil War and the division of the North from the South. However, the line was created to settle a boundary dispute in the young colonies. Astronomer Charles Mason and mathematician Jeremiah Dixon conducted the survey.

The survey settled a land dispute between the Calvert family of Maryland and the Penn family of Pennsylvania. The two families had been given their land by different English kings. But, the boundary lines of the land grants did not match. The families asked Mason and Dixon to mark a new boundary line. The survey took them nearly five years to complete.

Huge blocks of limestone, some weighing as much as 600 pounds (272 kg), were used as markers. The stones were brought from Great Britain. They were carried by wagons and placed at one-mile (1.6 km) intervals on the boundary line. Each mile marker was decorated with a *P* on the north face and an *M* on the south face. At every fifth mile, the marker was engraved with the Penn coat of arms on one side and the Calvert coat of arms on the other.

The boundary between the two states stretched for more than 233 miles (375 km). Mason and Dixon worked without modern equipment. They relied on the stars to calculate their path. Even so, recent Global Positioning System (GPS) technology proved that the line they marked was accurate. Amazingly, they were off by as little as a single inch (2.5 cm) in some places!

1. Which served as the best resource for Mason and Dixon as they worked to complete their survey?

    A.   historic maps of the region

    B.   conversations with area residents

    C.   the stars

    D.   GPS technology

2. Number the following events in the order in which they happened.

    _____ Mason and Dixon were hired to conduct the survey.

    _____ Mason and Dixon used limestone blocks to mark a new boundary line.

    _____ The Calvert and Penn families were locked in a boundary dispute.

    _____ Huge blocks of limestone were brought from England.

3. What is the setting for the passage?

    A.   eastern United States   B.   southern United States

    C.   England   D.   California

4. In what time period was the Mason-Dixon Line created?

    A.   before the Civil War   B.   during the Civil War

    C.   after the Civil War   D.   before the area was settled

5. Why was Mason and Dixon's survey necessary?

_____

_____

The Biggest Diamond

Read the passage. Then, answer the questions.

The world's largest rough-gem–quality diamond was discovered in 1905 in South Africa. The diamond was named the *Cullinan* after Sir Thomas Cullinan, the owner of the diamond mine.

A mine superintendent named Frederick Wells discovered the diamond as he was walking through the mine. When Wells noticed the large mass set in one side of the mine's wall, he thought it was a big piece of glass put there by a practical joker. When he examined it further, he realized that it was a huge diamond weighing 3,106 carats! Wells received a $10,000 bonus for his find.

The diamond was purchased for $800,000 as a gift for King Edward VII. The stone was sent to Amsterdam, where the Asscher Brothers were to cut it. The jewelers had a reputation for successfully cutting large diamonds. They studied the diamond for months. On the first attempt to cut the diamond, Joseph Asscher broke the blade. The diamond remained **intact**. On the second attempt, it split exactly as planned. After the second cut, Asscher reportedly fainted.

Further cuts produced three principal parts. These parts were then cut into nine major gems. Additional cuts produced 96 smaller brilliants and several carats of unpolished pieces. The *Cullinan I* was the largest gem cut from the rough stone. It is a pear-shaped stone of 530.2 carats and was the world's largest cut diamond at the time.

The *Cullinan I* is now in the head of the royal scepter in the British crown jewels and is on display in the Tower of London.

1. Based on the passage, which of the following units are used to measure the weight of diamonds?

   A. ounces   B. pounds

   C. grams   D. carats

2. Which of the following offers the best explanation for why Joseph Asscher may have fainted?

   A. He was tired from working a very long day.
   B. He was suffering from an undetected illness.
   C. He was relieved of the pressure of the task he had performed.
   D. He did not want to cut any more diamonds, so he faked an illness.

3. Number the following events in the order in which they happened.

   _____ Frederick Wells received a bonus of $10,000.

   _____ Sir Thomas Cullinan sold the diamond for $800,000.

   _____ The largest diamond is now a part of the British crown jewels.

   _____ Frederick Wells, a mine superintendent, found the huge diamond.

4. Which of the following best defines the word **intact**?

   A. without regard   B. not cared for
   C. whole   D. unavailable

5. What could be another title for this passage?

   _____

Boston Tea Party

Read the passage. Then, answer the questions.

Colonists who traveled to the New World often sought freedom and prosperity. Many colonists **allied** with the British troops during the French and Indian War. However, the colonists began to feel a greater independence from the British crown.

The cost of the French and Indian War left England in debt. After the war, King George III and the British Parliament began taxing the colonists to recover some of the war's costs and to regain control of the colonies. Many colonists became angry with the British government for taxing them without representation in Parliament.

The British Parliament's tax on imported tea angered the colonists the most. Tea was a staple of life for the colonists. Britain's East India Company owned large stocks of tea that it could not sell. Parliament granted the struggling company the right to export its tea to the colonies without paying a tax on the goods it sold. This would allow the company to **undersell** all of the colonial merchants. The colonists would be able to get their tea cheaper than before, but they would need to buy it from a British company.

This forced the colonists to pay a tax on the tea they bought and to recognize Parliament's right to tax them. The colonists realized the plan. To show their anger, about 150 colonists boarded the ships that carried the cargo of tea. During the night, they dumped all 342 chests of tea overboard into Boston Harbor, in what became known as the Boston Tea Party. Not long after, the colonists formally declared their independence from British rule.

1. What was the main source of the colonists' anger?

    A.   the outcome of the French and Indian War

    B.   being taxed without representation in Parliament

    C.   the personalities of the members of Parliament

    D.   being forced to drink tea

2. Which of the following best defines the word **allied**?

    A.   took the same side   B.   fought

    C.   agreed   D.   took a different side

3. Why did Parliament place a tax on imported tea?

    A.   to raise the money needed to give their soldiers a raise

    B.   to help the struggling colonists

    C.   to show the colonists that it had a right to impose taxes

    D.   to discourage the colonists from drinking tea

4. Write *T* if the statement is true. Write *F* if the statement is false.

    _____ Parliament imposed a tax on all imported food.

    _____ The British fought the French and Indian War.

    _____ About 150 colonists dumped tea into Chicago Harbor.

    _____ The East India Company exported its tea to the colonies without paying a tax to the British government on the goods it sold.

5. Which of the following best defines the word **undersell**?

    A.   to sell something for less money than everyone else

    B.   to sell the least amount of something

    C.   to have a shop below ground

    D.   to not be able to sell something

Dynamic Duo: Stanton and Anthony

Read the passage. Then, answer the questions.

Elizabeth Cady Stanton was an activist, a writer, an editor, and an **abolitionist**. In 1840, she went to the World Anti-Slavery Convention in London, England. While there, she was angered to find out that women were not recognized at the convention.

Stanton met with Lucretia Mott. The women planned a convention to improve women's rights. In 1848, they held their convention in Seneca Falls, New York. It helped start the equal rights movement for women. Stanton later developed a working relationship with Susan B. Anthony. The two made a great team. Stanton did not want to travel very much. So, Stanton wrote the speeches, and Anthony delivered them to the public.

The pair established the National Woman Suffrage Association. Stanton became its president. However, Anthony was always the better known of the pair. Her travels across the country made her familiar to many Americans. She devoted all of her efforts to winning women's **suffrage**, or the right to vote. Anthony made headlines when she was arrested for voting. She used the trial and the newspaper coverage to gain support for her cause.

Stanton, however, was involved in many different reforms. She worked to improve educational opportunities for women. She did not think that gaining the right to vote was more important than these other issues. Her autobiography, *Eighty Years and More,* was a huge success. Stanton continued to write about women's freedom and progress until her death in 1902.

1. What prompted Elizabeth Cady Stanton to organize a convention in Seneca Falls, New York?

_____

_____

_____

2. Why was Susan B. Anthony more well known than Elizabeth Cady Stanton?

   A. Anthony traveled more and saw more of the public.
   B. Anthony made the speeches.
   C. Stanton was the speechwriter and remained in the background much of the time.
   D. all of the above

3. Which best pinpoints the time setting for the passage?

   A. late eighteenth century   B. mid-1800s
   C. early 1800s   D. mid-1900s

4. Which of the following best defines the word **abolitionist**?

   A. someone concerned with climate change
   B. someone opposed to slavery
   C. someone opposed to equal rights for women
   D. someone who wanted voting rights for women

5. Which of the following best defines the word **suffrage**?

   A. a person who is suffering from great pain
   B. a person who does not feel pain
   C. the right to vote
   D. the right to free speech

Totem Poles

Read the passage. Then, answer the questions.

Many of the first explorers who saw totem poles called them "monstrous figures." Missionaries thought that the American Indians worshipped totem poles and encouraged the totem poles' destruction. But, the missionaries were wrong. Even today, many people do not understand totem poles. When people refer to the "low man on the totem pole," they do not realize that the largest figure was usually on the bottom and was the most important.

American Indian artists carved totem poles from cedar using handmade tools. The chisel was often made from an animal horn. The adze, which was like an ax, had a hard stone blade. After carving, the artist painted the totem poles with animal-hair brushes.

Totem poles told stories about rich and important American Indian families and sometimes included hidden meanings. American Indians celebrated an event—such as a birth or a marriage—with a feast, or *potlatch*. One of the highlights of the feast was the raising of a new totem pole.

In 1884, the Canadian government outlawed the potlatch. Not long after, the U.S. government followed suit. As children grew up and left their tribes, the art of carving totem poles began to die out.

Many years later, totem poles that had been bought or stolen from American Indian villages began to appear in museums. People started to realize the significance of totem poles, and the art of carving them was resurrected. Old totem poles were restored, and new ones were created. Today, the craft is alive and well again.

1. Which of the following best explains the purpose of totem poles?

   A. They could scare away enemy tribes.
   B. They were used as centerpieces in some religions.
   C. They told stories about important families.
   D. They were carved to keep European explorers guessing.

2. What was an ax-like tool used to carve totem poles?

   A. chisel   B. maul
   C. hammer   D. adze

3. Why did the art of carving totem poles fade during the 1800s?

   _____

   _____

   _____

4. What is the setting for the passage?

   A. The United States and Canada
   B. Southern California
   C. Northern Alaska and Russia
   D. The desert Southwest of the United States

5. What factors do you think were responsible for the revival of totem poles?

   _____

   _____

   _____

The Return of the Swallows

Read the passage. Then, answer the questions.

Every year, the Return of the Swallows celebration takes place on March 19 at the Mission San Juan Capistrano in California. That is the day people begin to look for the birds' return to the old complex of religious buildings. Visitors come from all over the world to celebrate the birds' arrival as a sign of the return of spring.

Where do the birds spend the winter months? **Ornithologists** have tracked them to Argentina. The birds are cliff swallows that have been returning to the area for centuries. The swallows build nests out of mud, and they return to these same nests each year. Nests that have survived the winter may need only minor repairs.

In his book, *Capistrano Nights*, Father St. John O'Sullivan tells the story of how the swallows first came to Capistrano. One day, the legend says, Father O'Sullivan saw a shopkeeper knocking down the swallows' nests with a broomstick. Supposedly, O'Sullivan invited the swallows to live at the mission. The next day, he found the swallows building their nests under the mission's eaves. The mission's location near the river was perfect. There was mud for the swallows to use in building their nests, and there were plenty of insects for food.

The swallows are Capistrano's most famous "citizens." They are protected by an ordinance that has made the entire city a bird sanctuary. Every October, the swallows return to Argentina for the winter. The cycle is completed each March when the first birds arrive at the mission.

1. Which of the following best defines the word **ornithologists**?

    A. Spanish mission priests

    B. bird-watchers

    C. scientists who study birds

    D. veterinarians specializing in birds

2. When do the swallows return to Capistrano?

    A. around February 1   B. around March 19

    C. around October 23   D. on Christmas Day

3. Where do the swallows go when they leave Capistrano?

    A. southern California   B. Venezuela

    C. southern Canada   D. Argentina

4. Why do people celebrate when the swallows return to Capistrano?

    A. The swallow is California's state bird.

    B. Everyone likes a reason to celebrate.

    C. The swallows bring good luck.

    D. People believe the swallows' return is a sign of the return of spring.

5. Why do you think the swallows chose the mission at San Juan Capistrano as the site to build their nests?

_____

_____

_____

The History of Cheese

Read the passage. Then, answer the questions.

Cheese finds its way onto sandwiches and crackers and into soups, casseroles, and salads. People who enjoy eating cheese may not realize it, but cheese has a long and mysterious history.

No one knows exactly when cheese was first created, but pictures of cheese makers can be found on the walls of Egyptian tombs dating back to 2000 BC. However, the Roman Empire is responsible for spreading cheese throughout the world. Because cheese could be carried long distances without spoiling, Roman soldiers took it with them on their travels to other lands.

To make cheese, milk must be mixed with **rennet**. Rennet is a digestive enzyme found in the stomachs of mammals. The acid in the rennet causes protein to clump together. These clumps, called *curds*, form cheese. What happens to the curds next determines the flavor and texture of the cheese. Some curds are heated to high temperatures, some have salts added to them, and some are allowed to sit so that mold will grow on them. In fact, there are more than 1,000 different types of cheese.

Cheese was probably created by accident. Legend has it that a Middle Eastern merchant discovered cheese when he took milk with him on a journey. He put the milk in a bag made from a sheep's stomach, which contained rennet. As he walked, the two ingredients mixed together. The next time he went to drink milk from the bag, he found cheese!

1. Write *T* if the statement is true. Write *F* if the statement is false.

_____ Roman soldiers took cheese with them on their travels.

_____ An Egyptian pharaoh discovered cheese in 2000 BC.

_____ Some cheeses are heated to high temperatures to give them a specific flavor.

_____ There are more than 1,000 different types of cheese.

2. Which of the following best defines the word **rennet**?
   A. the digestion of milk by mammals
   B. the process of heating cheese to high temperatures to kill bacteria
   C. a type of cheese produced in the Middle East
   D. an enzyme that is used to make cheese

3. Which of the following best describes the main idea of the passage?
   A. According to legend, the first person to discover cheese was a merchant in the Middle East.
   B. There are hundreds of different types of cheese.
   C. No one knows for sure how cheese was discovered, but cheese has a long and interesting history.
   D. It took years to discover cheese.

4. Which of the following is another good title for the passage?
   A. An Accidental Discovery
   B. The Many Varieties of Cheese
   C. According to Legend
   D. What Would We Do Without Cheese?

Halley's Comet

Read the passage. Then, answer the questions.

Halley's comet was named after astronomer Edmond Halley. Halley had a theory that comets were natural **phenomena** of the solar system. He believed comets orbited the sun. He said that one particular comet's orbit would take about 76 years to complete. Halley's research showed that the comet had been observed for centuries. He found evidence that the comet passed Earth in the years 1531, 1607, and 1682.

Halley predicted that the comet would return in 1758. His prediction came true. The comet was named in his honor. Halley's comet makes regular visits to Earth. Various forces combine to make the comet's orbit take about 76 years. However, the gravitational pull of the planets can change the path of the orbit, which can alter the length of time of the orbit. The comet's orbit has taken as long as 79 years. Halley's comet is expected to return to Earth in 2061.

Modern scientists wondered about the comet's makeup. In 1985, they launched the spacecraft *Giotto*. Its mission was to take pictures of Halley's comet as it passed Earth. The pictures were taken from only 372.8 miles (600 km) away from the comet. This was the closest any camera had ever been to observe Halley's comet.

Giotto sent valuable data back to scientists. The core of the comet is about 9 miles (15 km) long. It is very dark and porous. The core is made up of equal amounts of dust and ice. Scientists also determined that Halley's comet formed about 4.5 billion years ago.

1. Why is Halley's comet so well known?

   A. because of the size of its core
   B. because of its fairly regular orbital pattern
   C. because of its composition of ice turned to dust
   D. because of its beauty

2. About how often does Halley's comet visit Earth?

   A. every 76 years   B. every 89 years
   C. every year   D. once every other century

3. About how long is the core of Halley's comet?

   A. 90 miles (144.8 km)   B. 900 miles (1,448.4 km)
   C. 19 miles (30.6 km)   D. 9 miles (15 km)

4. Which of the following best defines the word **phenomena**?

   A. comets with predictable orbits
   B. observable facts or events
   C. routine conditioning
   D. expectations

5. What causes the orbit of Halley's comet to vary slightly in length?

   _____

   _____

   _____

Maris's Baseball Record

Read the passage. Then, answer the questions.

On October 1, 1961, Roger Maris of the New York Yankees hit his 61st home run of the season. His home run broke the record set by the legendary Babe Ruth. Ruth hit 60 home runs during the 1927 season. Baseball fans were not quick to let go of the magic that accompanied Ruth's record.

Maris had been the 1960 American League's Most Valuable Player. He was a gifted right fielder and an excellent base runner. In spite of this, he was virtually unknown. Maris was a fierce competitor, and he was determined to break Ruth's record. His more popular teammate, Mickey Mantle, was also chasing the record and was the crowd favorite.

In 1961, as more teams joined the league, the season was expanded from 154 games to 162. The baseball commissioner, Ford Frick, decided that if Maris took more than 154 games to break the record, it would be listed in the record books as a separate accomplishment. Many fans agreed with Frick's decision.

The Yankees considered switching Maris, who batted third, and Mantle, who batted fourth. This change would have given Mantle a better shot at breaking Ruth's record. However, in September, Mantle suffered a hip injury and missed several games. Maris continued his **torrid** pace. When he approached his 154th game, he had 58 home runs. He hit number 59 in that game. Maris broke the record on the last day of the season in the 162nd game.

1. Why were fans reluctant to root for Roger Maris to break Babe Ruth's home run record?

    A. Roger Maris was not well known.
    B. Mickey Mantle, who was also chasing Ruth's record, was a more popular player.
    C. Baseball fans did not want to let go of the magic of Ruth's record.
    D. all of the above

2. Why was the baseball season increased to 162 games?

    A. Baseball players wanted to play more games.
    B. Baseball fans had asked for a longer season.
    C. The league had added more teams, so more games were added.
    D. none of the above

3. What could be another title for the passage?

    _____

4. Do you think it was fair to place Roger Maris's record in a separate category so that Babe Ruth's record could stand? Why or why not?

    _____

    _____

    _____

5. Which of the following best defines the word **torrid**?

    A. torn   B. steady
    C. irregular   D. very hot; fast

The Ides of March

Read the passage. Then, answer the questions.

William Shakespeare **immortalized** the phrase "ides of March" in his play *Julius Caesar*. During the play, Caesar asks a soothsayer (or fortune-teller) what his future holds. He is told to "Beware the ides of March!" This line from Shakespeare is likely the reason that we still say "ides of March" today. What exactly are the ides, and why was Caesar told to beware?

The "ides of March" is a phrase meaning the "15th of March." It comes from the ancient Romans. The Roman calendar built its months around three types of days. Those days were called *calends* (the first day of the month), *nones* (the seventh day of the month), and *ides* (either the 13th or 15th day of the month). In March, May, July, and October, the ides fell on the 15th day of the month. The ides were on the 13th day in all of the other months. Romans identified the other days of the month by counting backward or forward from the calends, nones, or ides. For example, a Roman would refer to the 18th of a month as, "three days after the ides."

Every month had an ides. However, the ides of March has historical significance. Julius Caesar died in 44 BC on the 15th of March. That is why the soothsayer in the play told Caesar to "beware the ides of March!"

Aside from the ides of March, the Roman calendar provided the basis for our modern calendar system of 365 days in a year and 366 days in a leap year. The Romans are also responsible for the word *calendar*, which comes from the word *calends*.

1. On which day of the month might the ides fall?

    A. the first day of the month
    B. the seventh day of the month
    C. the last day of the month
    D. the 15th day of the month

2. Which of the following best defines the word **immortalized**?

    A. explained clearly   B. accented
    C. made to last forever   D. told the future

3. Why did the soothsayer tell Caesar to "Beware the ides of March!" in Shakespeare's play?

    A. He was foreshadowing Caesar's death.
    B. He had met Caesar before, and he did not like him.
    C. He was addressing a very important man.
    D. He was concerned about Caesar's outstanding debts.

4. What is the main idea of the passage?

    A. The Roman calendar only had three days.
    B. Julius Caesar was died on the ides of March.
    C. The ides of March is a term that we remember because of Shakespeare and Julius Caesar.
    D. The ides of March has always been a superstitious day.

5. Do you think the Roman calendar is complicated? Why or why not?

    _____

    _____

    _____

Pat Mora

Read the passage. Then, answer the questions.

Pat Mora grew up in El Paso, Texas, near the border of the United States and Mexico. Her parents saw that she had a talent for words, but Mora did not write much as a child. Both Mora's teachers and parents supported her talent. They influenced her love of poetry from a young age. Then, when she neared the age of 40, Mora started to write poetry and stories.

Mora is proud to be both a Hispanic woman and an American. She writes in English but uses Spanish words throughout her stories and poems to honor her Mexican heritage. Many of her books take place in the southwestern United States.

One of Mora's favorite things to do is visit schools and share what she calls "bookjoy," the great feeling of reading and learning new things. Reading was always important to her, so she wants students to love reading too. Mora also helped bring a Mexican tradition to the United States. In 1996, she learned that April 30 is the Day of the Child in Mexico. In the United States, Mora linked this day to children's books and reading. Now, libraries and schools in 15 states celebrate this day, thanks to her hard work. Someday, Mora hopes to bring this day of bookjoy to everyone in the country.

1. What is the first paragraph mainly about?

   A. how Mora started to write
   B. why Mora likes to visit schools
   C. one of Mora's books
   D. how Mora was first published

2. Write *T* if the statement is true. Write *F* if the statement is false.

   _____ Mora started writing songs when she was 40 years old.

   _____ Mora's poetry uses both English and Spanish words.

   _____ Mora grew up in the northwestern United States.

   _____ Mora believes in "bookjoy," the great feeling of reading and learning new things.

   _____ Mora brought the Day of the Child to the United States.

3. Why do you think Mora likes to visit schools?

   _____

   _____

   _____

4. Which of the following is Mora's way of honoring her Mexican heritage?

   A. She writes poetry and books for children.
   B. Many of her stories are about Mexico.
   C. She uses Spanish words in her poems and stories.
   D. all of the above

Presidential Impeachment

Read the passage. Then, draw a line to match each word to the correct definition.

If the president of the United States does something illegal, the House of Representatives can vote to impeach him. To impeach a president means to charge him with a crime. The majority of the members of the House of Representatives must vote to impeach a president. Next, the Senate has a trial to decide whether the president is guilty. The Chief Justice of the Supreme Court presides over the trial. The senators take the role of the jury. Two-thirds of the Senate must vote guilty for the president to be convicted. If a president is found guilty, he is removed from office. He can no longer be the president. Only two presidents have ever been impeached: Andrew Johnson and Bill Clinton. Neither was convicted by Congress, and neither lost his job.

1. impeach

A. a group of people who decide if a person is guilty of a crime

2. illegal

B. more than half

3. majority

C. a job, usually in public service

4. preside

D. to charge the president with a crime

5. convicted

E. not allowed by law

6. jury

F. proven guilty

7. office

G. to be in charge; oversee

8. charge

H. to accuse someone of a crime

Emily Dickinson

Read the passage and poem. Then, answer the questions.

Emily Dickinson is one of the most famous American poets. However, during her lifetime, she was nearly unknown. She wrote about 1,800 poems. Fewer than a dozen were published before her death. Today, Dickinson is known for her unusual use of capital letters and punctuation. Vivid imagery, **slant rhyme**, and broken meter are also well-known characteristics of her poetry. She did not give her poems titles. Scholars assigned numbers to Dickinson's poems. They are often organized in order based on when scholars think that each poem was written.

254

"Hope" is the thing with feathers –
That perches in the soul –
And sings the tune without the words –
And never stops – at all –

And sweetest – in the Gale – is heard –
And sore must be the storm –
That could **abash** the little Bird
That kept so many warm –

I've heard it in the chillest land –
And on the strangest Sea –
Yet, never, in Extremity,
It asked a crumb – of Me.

1. To what does Emily Dickinson compare hope?

    A.   a song   B.   a bird

    C.   a strong wind   D.   all of the above

2. Which of the following best defines the word **abash**?

    A.   to make a loud sound   B.   to feel cold or sleepy

    C.   to sing softly   D.   to unsettle or embarrass

3. What do you think Dickinson means when she writes that hope is "sweetest – in the Gale"?

_____

_____

_____

4. When words sound similar but do not rhyme exactly, it is called **slant rhyme**. Find two pairs of slant rhymes in the poem and write them in the spaces below.

_____ / _____

_____ / _____

5. Dickinson is famous for her sporadic use of dashes and punctuation, slant rhymes, unusual capitalization, and broken meter. How do these characteristics affect the way you read the poem?

_____

_____

Mardi Gras

Read the passage. Then, answer the questions.

The term *Mardi Gras* ("mär-dē grä") is French for "Fat Tuesday." It is the last day of the carnival festivities before Lent. The next day is Ash Wednesday, which marks the beginning of Lent. Over time, Mardi Gras has come to represent the entire carnival period. One of the biggest celebrations takes place in New Orleans, Louisiana.

The French were holding masked balls and costume parties in New Orleans as early as 1718. When the Spanish government rose to power, parties were banned. After the Spanish rule ended, people could once again attend parties and hide their identities behind masks. During the 1850s, the elegant Mardi Gras parties continued but were in contrast to wild parties going on in the streets. The celebration was in danger of being banned again.

In 1857, a group of men formed a secret society called the Mystick Krewe of Comus. They wanted to save Mardi Gras with proper planning and management. So, they planned the first Mardi Gras parade. Next, the Krewe of Rex was formed to celebrate the arrival of visiting royalty from Russia. Because America did not have royalty, the men in Rex created their own "king for a day," secretly choosing one of their members to be the king of the carnival. This idea quickly caught on with other Mardi Gras **krewes**.

Since then, many other secret societies have been established in New Orleans. Because the krewes pay for all of the parades, Mardi Gras has been called the "Greatest Free Show on Earth." The celebration attracts millions of visitors every year.

1. Which of the following best defines the word **krewes**?

   A. men's sweaters B. staff members on a ship

   C. secret societies D. close-shaven haircuts

2. When does the Mardi Gras celebration begin each year?

   A. on the first day of spring

   B. before Ash Wednesday

   C. right after Fat Tuesday

   D. on the first day of summer

3. The roots of Mardi Gras can be traced to which country's heritage?

   A. Russia B. France

   C. Germany D. Italy

4. Why do some people wear masks and costumes during the festivities?

   A. to hide their identities

   B. to make the parades more exciting

   C. because the mayor of New Orleans issued a decree

   D. because the masks are pretty

5. What was the Mystick Krewe of Comus?

   _____

   _____

   _____

Read the movie times. Then, use the schedule to answer the questions.

Summer Movies
Afternoon and Evening Schedule

Cinema 6

Oceans Apart
12:30 2:15 4:30

Land of Treasure
12:15 2:30 5:00

Gridiron Greats
1:00 3:00 5:30

Super Safari
1:00 3:30 6:00

Feline Friends
12:30 2:45 5:00

Your Lucky Day
12:00 3:30

The Prairie Pals
12:00 3:30 6:15

Movie Mania

Your Lucky Day
12:30 2:15 4:30
7:00

Land of Treasure
12:15 2:45 5:30
7:30

Gridiron Greats
1:30 4:00

Super Safari
12:30 5:30

Oceans Apart
3:30 6:00

Theater Town

Feline Friends
1:00 3:30 5:00

Gridiron Greats
1:00 3:15 5:30

Time and Time Again
12:30 3:45 6:15

Your Lucky Day
12:15 3:00 5:00

The Prairie Pals
2:00 5:15

Land of Treasure
12:00 3:45 6:30

1. Which movie has the latest showtime of all?

   A. *The Prairie Pals*   B. *Super Safari*
   C. *Land of Treasure*   D. *Gridiron Greats*

2. Jamie has a scout meeting at 4:00 P.M. Her family would like to see a movie before the meeting. Which of the following movies should her family *not* watch?

   A. *Oceans Apart* at Movie Mania
   B. *Gridiron Greats* at Theater Town
   C. *Your Lucky Day* at Cinema 6
   D. *Super Safari* at Movie Mania

3. Three children are in the Sanchez family. Each child wants to see a different movie. Which theater is showing three different movies with the same starting time?

   _____

4. How are the movies on this schedule organized?

   A. by the name of the theater where the movie will be shown
   B. alphabetically by the name of the movie
   C. by the time of day the movie will be shown
   D. by the number of times the movie will be shown per day

The Great Chicago Fire

Read the passage. Then, answer the questions.

Experts agree that the Great Chicago Fire started in or near the barn of Catherine O'Leary on Sunday evening, October 8, 1871. The fire finally burned out on the morning of October 10. By then, the fire had cut a path through about three square miles (7.8 square km) of downtown Chicago, Illinois. Property damage was nearly $200 million. More than 90,000 people were left homeless. What experts disagree about is how the fire started.

Urban legend says that the fire started when Mrs. O'Leary's cow kicked over a lantern. Supposedly, Mrs. O'Leary used the lantern to provide light as she milked her cow. This story first appeared in the *Chicago Evening Journal*. But, Mrs. O'Leary denied causing the fire.

An inquiry into the origin of the fire involved talking to more than 50 people and recording hundreds of pages of testimony. No agreement was ever reached on the cause of the fire.

Some said Daniel Sullivan started the fire. His **inconsistent** testimony led people to think that he was the culprit. Other people believed that his neighbor, Dennis Regan, might have been an accomplice. Regan's testimony was also inconsistent. Their strange behavior and comments made it seem that they were in some way responsible.

No one can be sure how the fire started. However, some who are familiar with the matter think that people should stop blaming Mrs. O'Leary's cow.

1. Number the following events in the order in which they happened.

    _____ Daniel Sullivan gave some inconsistent testimony.

    _____ The fire destroyed Mrs. O'Leary's barn and much of downtown Chicago.

    _____ The Great Chicago Fire started on October 8, 1871.

    _____ An inquiry was launched into the cause of the fire.

2. Which of the following best defines the word **inconsistent**?
    A. confusing
    B. contrary to popular belief
    C. not compatible with another fact, claim, or statement
    D. without justification or truth

3. Write O if the statement is an opinion. Write F if the statement is a fact.

    _____ Mrs. O'Leary's cow should not be blamed for causing the Great Chicago Fire.

    _____ Daniel Sullivan probably caused the Great Chicago Fire.

    _____ The Great Chicago Fire left more than 90,000 people homeless.

    _____ Lanterns do not belong in barns.

Ella Fitzgerald

Read the passage. Then, answer the questions.

At 16 years old, Ella Fitzgerald performed at Harlem's Apollo Theater. She had no idea that her life was about to change. Her childhood had been hard. After the death of her parents, Fitzgerald went to boarding school. She ran away when the teachers mistreated her. Homeless, she struggled to survive on the streets of New York City. In 1934, she won a contest to perform during amateur night at the Apollo. She sang her mother's favorite song, and her performance earned her respect from several well-known musicians. Fitzgerald went on to become a **renowned** jazz singer.

Fitzgerald's musical career spanned six decades. During that time, she released more than 200 albums. She won 13 Grammy awards. She received her last Grammy in 1990. Fitzgerald worked with some of the greatest American singers of the twentieth century, including Frank Sinatra, Louis Armstrong, Count Basie, and Dizzy Gillespie. Her talent and charm pleased a wide range of listeners around the world and helped make jazz a more popular genre.

Fitzgerald never took her success for granted. She gave money to charities that cared for needy children. In 1992, she received the Presidential Medal of Freedom, one of the highest honors available to civilians.

In 1991, Ella Fitzgerald gave her final performance in New York's Carnegie Hall. She died in 1996. However, the American "First Lady of Song" continues to live in the hearts of music lovers worldwide.

1. Which of the following best defines the word **renowned**?

   A. wealthy   B. talented

   C. famous   D. underappreciated

2. Number the following events in the order in which they happened.

   _____ Fitzgerald won a contest to perform during amateur night at the Apollo Theater in New York City.

   _____ Fitzgerald was orphaned and placed in a boarding school.

   _____ Fitzgerald received the Presidential Medal of Freedom.

   _____ Fitzgerald gave her final performance.

   _____ Fitzgerald received her final Grammy award.

3. How did Fitzgerald help make jazz a more popular musical genre?

   A. She advertised on TV.
   B. Her talent and charm appealed to listeners around the world.
   C. She often sang duets with unknown musicians so that they could also become famous.
   D. none of the above

4. Why do you think Ella Fitzgerald is called the "First Lady of Song"?

   _____

   _____

   _____

The Pentagon

Read the passage. Then, answer the questions.

The Pentagon is the headquarters for the U.S. Department of Defense. It is one of the world's largest office buildings. More than 23,000 employees work there on a daily basis. Their jobs are to plan and carry out a safe defense for the United States.

The site of the Pentagon was originally swampland. Construction was finished in only 16 months, and the building was dedicated in 1943. It cost nearly $83 million to build. The building consolidated War Department work being done in 17 separate buildings scattered around Washington, D.C.

The Pentagon is one of the most efficient buildings in the world. It has more than 17 miles (27 km) of corridors. However, it takes only seven minutes to walk between any two points in the building. Employees park nearly 9,000 cars in 16 parking lots. They climb 131 stairways and ride 13 elevators or 19 escalators to their offices.

The Pentagon has five main floors called **mezzanines**, as well as two basements. Five concentric rings are connected by 10 spoke-like corridors. The five-sided design was chosen because of the five existing roads surrounding the original site.

1. Which of the following statements best explains why the Pentagon is a five-sided building?

   A. It was built to resemble a star with five points.
   B. Five roads surround the original site of the building.
   C. Each side represents a branch of the military service.
   D. The architect came up with a new and unusual plan.

2. Write *T* if the statement is true. Write *F* if the statement is false.

   _____ The Pentagon has more than 17 miles (27 km) of corridors.

   _____ Fewer than 23,000 employees work in the Pentagon.

   _____ The cost of the Pentagon was more than $25 million.

   _____ The Pentagon is one of the world's largest office buildings.

3. Which of the following best defines the word **mezzanines**?

   A. supply charts
   B. basement additions
   C. low stories or main floors in a building
   D. winding hallways

4. Why has the Pentagon been described as one of the most efficient office buildings in the world?

   _____

   _____

   _____

Miracle Mets

Read the passage. Then, answer the questions.

The expansion New York Mets baseball **franchise** first took the field in 1962. As often happens with expansion teams, fans did not expect much during the first few years. A new franchise usually starts at the bottom of the league. Draft choices are made, and key players need to be acquired. It usually takes a while before a new team has all of the right elements to be successful.

The Mets fell into this role perfectly. Unfortunately, they stayed there too long. They were so terrible that fans called them "lovable losers." Fans continued to come to the stadium, though, because the Mets were fun to watch.

Through their first seven seasons, the Mets never finished higher than ninth place. During spring training in 1969, catcher Jerry Grote told his teammates that the Mets would win the World Series that season. His teammates laughed. Surprisingly, Grote's prediction came true.

A winning streak at the end of that season enabled the Mets to win the Eastern Division title. Then, they defeated the Atlanta Braves to win the National League pennant. In the World Series, they faced the Baltimore Orioles. The Mets lost the first game in Baltimore. However, they won the second game and returned to New York tied with the Orioles at one game each.

The "Miracle Mets" won the next three games to win the 1969 World Series four games to one. The Mets shocked the sporting world with one of the most incredible seasons ever.

1. Write *T* if the statement is true. Write *F* if the statement is false.

_____ The Mets won the World Series in their first year of baseball.

_____ Fans loved the Mets even when they lost.

_____ The Mets won the Eastern Division title in 1969.

_____ The Mets won the 1969 World Series four games to one.

2. What is the setting for the passage?
   A. New York, New York
   B. Los Angeles, California
   C. Atlanta, Georgia
   D. Baltimore, Maryland

3. Which of the following best defines the word **franchise**?
   A. right of membership in a professional sports league
   B. agreement between league officials
   C. official team logo
   D. team payroll for the players and managers

4. Number the following events in the order in which they happened.

_____ The Mets defeated the Baltimore Orioles four games to one.

_____ The Mets defeated the Atlanta Braves to win the National League pennant.

_____ The Mets won the Eastern Division title.

_____ The Mets won the World Series of baseball.

An African Trickster Tale

Read the story. Then, answer the questions.

In the beginning, people could not solve their problems. Nyame, the sky god, looked down and felt sorry for them. He said, "I will send wisdom to the people." Anansi, the spider man, overheard Nyame's plan. He said, "That is a good idea. Give the wisdom to me, and I will take it down to the people."

Nyame trusted the selfish trickster. He put his wisdom in a pot and gave it to Anansi. "This wisdom is more valuable than gold or silver," Nyame said.

Anansi took the pot down to Earth. It was full of wonderful ideas and skills. Anansi said greedily, "This wisdom is too valuable to share. I must keep it all to myself." He decided to hide the pot in the top of a tall tree. But, how could he get it there?

Anansi tied some strong vines around the pot and tied the other end around his waist. He started to climb, but the dangling pot kept getting caught in the branches. Anansi's young son saw his father's struggle. "Father," the boy said, "if you tie the pot to your back, it will be much easier for you to hold on to the tree and climb." Anansi followed his son's advice and made it to the top.

Suddenly he thought, *What a fool I am! I have the pot of wisdom, yet a little boy had more common sense than I did!* Anansi angrily threw the pot, and it smashed into millions of pieces. The wisdom scattered all over the world. People found bits of the wisdom and took them home to their families. That is why, when we exchange ideas, we share wisdom with each other.

1. Number the following events in the order in which they happened.

   _____ Anansi brought the pot of wisdom to Earth.

   _____ Nyame decided to give wisdom to people.

   _____ Anansi decided to keep the wisdom for himself.

   _____ People collected the wisdom and began to share it.

   _____ Anansi threw the pot of wisdom and it smashed into pieces.

2. How is Anansi described in the story?

   _____

3. Which of the following words best describes the story's genre?

   A. myth   B. novel
   C. history   D. epic

4. What is the main idea of the story?

   A. Wisdom belongs only to sneaky people.
   B. Wisdom is a heavy burden to carry.
   C. No one person has all of the wisdom in the world.
   D. Parents should always follow their children's advice.

5. For centuries, people around the world have told trickster tales to explain human behavior. What human behavior does this story try to explain?

   _____

   _____

   _____

A Lady

Read the poem. Then, answer the questions.

A lady wore a hat to the town's parade.
It had a big, red flower **perched** on top.
I saw her somewhere later, drinking lemonade;
I guess she prefers it to plain old soda pop.

She did look peculiar in her flowered hat;
I'd never ever seen anything like it before.
She also had a bag in which she carried her cat.
She stood smiling in front of Mr. Martin's store.

Then, two days later, I saw her wear a sock.
I think it was pink with big red polka dots.
She looked a little funny, but it wasn't quite a shock.
I guess she likes to dress up and visit town a lot!

1. Which of the following best defines the word **perched**?

    A. grown
    B. sitting on
    C. woven
    D. colored

2. Which word best describes the lady in the poem?

    A. typical
    B. shy
    C. unusual
    D. mean

3. What did the lady carry in her bag?

    _____

4. Write *O* if the statement is an opinion. Write *F* if the statement is a fact.

    _____ The lady's hat had a red flower.

    _____ The lady carried her cat in a bag.

    _____ The lady looked peculiar in her flowered hat.

    _____ The lady drank lemonade.

5. A rhyme scheme is a pattern of rhyming words in a poem. What is the rhyme scheme of "A Lady"?

    _____

Sue Hendrickson

Read the passage. Then, answer the questions.

As a child, Sue Hendrickson loved to look for buried treasure. She would also stroll along sidewalks, looking at the ground and hoping to find interesting things.

One day, Hendrickson visited an amber mine. One piece of amber had an insect trapped inside of it, and a miner told her that it was 23 million years old. At that moment, Hendrickson knew that she wanted to search for fossils.

In 1990, she traveled to South Dakota with a team of scientists looking for dinosaur bones. The team's truck had a flat tire. When the others went to get the tire fixed, Hendrickson and her dog stayed behind and went for a walk. On her walk, Hendrickson saw some bones on the ground and then looked up. There, in the sandstone cliff, was a huge dinosaur skeleton! The group uncovered the biggest, most complete skeleton of a *Tyrannosaurus rex* that had ever been found. The *T. rex* was named "Sue" after its discoverer.

This was not Hendrickson's only adventure. Two years later, she dove with scientists to explore a sunken ship. It was a Spanish trading ship from the 1600s. At the wreck, the scientists found hundreds of huge stone jars and more than 400 gold and silver coins.

Hendrickson has plans for more adventures. She wants to look for more dinosaur bones and hopes to find a woolly mammoth skeleton. Often, Hendrickson travels to the Field Museum in Chicago, Illinois, her hometown. That is where Sue the *T. rex* is on display. Sue Hendrickson likes to visit Sue the dinosaur whenever she can.

1. Which word best describes Sue Hendrickson?

   A. stern
   B. adventurous
   C. quiet
   D. funny

2. Number the following events in the order in which they happened.

   _____ Hendrickson grew up in Chicago, Illinois.

   _____ Hendrickson found a *T. rex* skeleton in South Dakota.

   _____ Hendrickson dove to explore a Spanish trading ship.

   _____ Hendrickson saw a piece of amber 23 million years old with an insect trapped inside.

   _____ Hendrickson wants to look for a woolly mammoth skeleton.

3. What year did Hendrickson dive with scientists to explore a sunken Spanish trading ship?

   _____

4. How did Hendrickson find the *T. rex* bones?

   A. She was digging with scientists when they all found the skeleton.
   B. Her dog found the bones and ran back to get her.
   C. She went for a walk while she was waiting for a flat tire to be fixed.
   D. She dove into the ocean looking for a sunken ship.

The Mayflower Compact

Read the passage. Then, write *O* if the statement is an opinion. Write *F* if the statement is a fact.

The Pilgrims were a group of people who disagreed with how the Church of England was run. They wanted to go to a place where they could establish their own church. They received permission to travel to England's Virginia colony in present-day America. There, they could worship as they pleased.

In September 1620, 102 settlers set sail for America on a ship called the *Mayflower*. The group consisted of Pilgrims and other Englishmen, whom the Pilgrims called "Strangers." In November, the ship arrived in present-day Massachusetts. The water to the south was too rough and dangerous, so they decided to stay where they were.

Some of the Strangers talked about leaving the group. But, the group believed they had a better chance of survival if they all stuck together. They had a better chance of success if they agreed to follow certain rules. So, they wrote an agreement called the *Mayflower Compact*. The document included laws and details about their government. All who signed promised to follow these laws.

Many people consider the Mayflower Compact to be the first form of self-government in America's history. Forty-one men, but no women, signed the compact. Women did not have many rights at that time and were not allowed to sign the compact. The men elected John Carver as their first governor, and they decided to settle in present-day Plymouth, Massachusetts.

1. _____ The Pilgrims' ideas about the church were better than England's ideas.

2. _____ The *Mayflower* sailed in 1620.

3. _____ Signing the Mayflower Compact was a good idea.

4. _____ Forty-one men signed the Mayflower Compact.

5. _____ John Carver was the smartest person on the *Mayflower*.

6. _____ About 102 people traveled to America on the *Mayflower*.

7. _____ The *Mayflower* did not land where the Pilgrims had first planned.

8. _____ The Mayflower Compact was a perfect agreement.

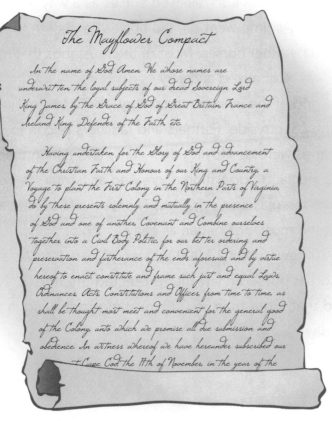

Mustangs

Read the passage. Then, answer the questions.

The image of horses running free across the plains is a popular symbol of the American West. However, mustangs are not **indigenous** to the United States. When Spanish armies came to the New World in the sixteenth century, they brought horses with them. Before the Spanish arrived, horses had been extinct in the Western hemisphere for about 12,000 years.

The free horses that live in the western United States are called *mustangs*. The word comes from the Spanish word *mesteño*, meaning "wild" or "stray." These horses escaped from the Spanish soldiers. Native tribes also released horses as a way to combat the Spanish army. As time went on, the horses gave birth to foals and were joined by other horses. Most of the mustangs that roam the plains today are of mixed ancestry.

By the end of the nineteenth century, about two million mustangs roamed the countryside. Farmers and ranchers began to complain. The mustangs were destroying their crops and eating their livestock's food. The mustang population decreased as farmers removed the horses from the plains and prairies. Then, private conservation efforts to protect the mustangs began as early as 1925.

By 1970, fewer than 17,000 mustangs were left. As a result, the U.S. Congress passed a law that protected the horses. Now, it is estimated that more than 35,000 mustangs are living in the United States today.

1. Which of the following best defines the word **indigenous**?

   A. a popular symbol

   B. a breed of horse

   C. native to an area

   D. from another country

2. Number the following events in the order in which they happened.

   _____ About two million mustangs roamed the countryside.

   _____ Spanish armies brought horses to the New World.

   _____ Congress passed a law protecting mustangs.

   _____ Horses became extinct in the Western hemisphere.

   _____ Private conservation efforts began to protect the mustangs.

3. Write *T* if the statement is true. Write *F* if the statement is false.

   _____ Today's mustangs are of pure Spanish ancestry.

   _____ Mustangs have always lived in North America.

   _____ The first mustangs escaped from the Spanish army.

   _____ Mustangs have always been a protected species in the United States.

4. Which of the following is another good title for the passage?

   A. Join the Herd

   B. Horsing Around

   C. Happy and Free

   D. Wild Horses of the West

Eleanor Roosevelt

Read the passage. Then, answer the questions.

Eleanor Roosevelt is often described as one of the most influential first ladies in American history. However, as a child, Eleanor Roosevelt was lonely and shy. She viewed herself as plain and felt she disappointed her mother. Her father adored her, but he was often gone. By age 10, Eleanor Roosevelt was an orphan.

As a teenager, Eleanor Roosevelt attended a boarding school in England. There, she met a teacher who helped her gain self-confidence. When she returned to the United States, she began her career as a human rights activist.

In 1905, Eleanor married Franklin Delano Roosevelt. Franklin was an intelligent, young politician. Together, they raised five children. In 1921, Franklin caught polio. Eleanor became his political eyes and ears. She visited people all over the nation. She learned about their problems and reported them to her husband. She also became active in political groups. She was a member of the women's division of the New York State Democratic Committee.

Franklin Delano Roosevelt became president in 1933. Eleanor changed the role of the first lady. Unlike her **predecessors**, she held press conferences. She also traveled, lectured, spoke on the radio, and wrote a daily newspaper column. Eleanor also worked to improve the lives of poor and needy people. She fought for women's rights and supported the civil rights movement.

After President Roosevelt's death, Eleanor became an American delegate to the United Nations. She had come a long way from the shy girl she used to be.

1. Which of the following best defines the word **predecessors**?

    A. the first people to ever do something
    B. people who perform their jobs well
    C. the people who previously held a particular job
    D. people who are currently in charge

2. Write four ways in which Eleanor changed the role of first lady.

    _____

    _____

    _____

    _____

3. Eleanor became the "political eyes and ears" of Franklin Delano Roosevelt. What does that phrase mean?

    A. Eleanor bought the president glasses and a hearing aid.
    B. Eleanor watched and listened to people for the president.
    C. Eleanor wore glasses and listened well.
    D. Eleanor did the president's job for him.

4. Number the following events in the order in which they happened.

    _____ Eleanor was an American delegate to the United Nations.

    _____ Eleanor attended boarding school in England.

    _____ Eleanor married Franklin Delano Roosevelt.

    _____ Eleanor became an orphan.

    _____ Eleanor changed the role of first lady.

In the Blink of an Eye

Read the passage. Then, answer the questions.

A person blinks about 12 times per minute on average during the waking hours of every day. If a person gets eight hours of sleep each night, then the person is awake for 16 hours each day. These statistics translate into about 11,520 blinks each day of our lives!

Our eyelids function much like the windshield wipers on a car. Eyelids are made of folds of skin that are raised and lowered by muscles. They move quickly so that our vision is not impaired. This is all done automatically. Why do we blink, and why is blinking so important?

One reason has to do with our eyelashes. Most of the eye is enclosed in a bony socket that is covered with a layer of fat to form a protective cover. However, when the eyes are open, a part of the surface area is exposed. The eyelashes help keep dust and other foreign particles from entering the eye.

Our eyes are also being cleansed and lubricated during the process of blinking. Every time an eyelid blinks, a mixture of oils, tears, and mucus, called a **tear film**, washes across the surface of the eye. This mixture moistens the eye and rinses away particles of dust and other matter that could cause irritation. The many glands that line the edge of each eyelid produce the oily component of the tear film. This oil keeps the tears from evaporating too quickly. Each eye also has a tear gland, which produces the tears that keep the eye comfortable and hydrated. If we do not blink often enough, or if too few tears are produced, our eyes feel dry and scratchy.